Specky and His Magical Spin-Oculars

Meet My Friends

Written by Tweedy Katz

Illustrated by Tweedy Katz & Leslie Braginsky

Published by

Tweed K LLC

BOCA RATON, FLORIDA

ISBN: 978-0-9994843-1-9
LCCN: 2017915909

For my Grandchildren.
Thank you for sharing your favorite
characters with me.

Dylan, Chase, Alec, Sydney,
Jonah, and Lucy.
Lots of Love!

SPECKY

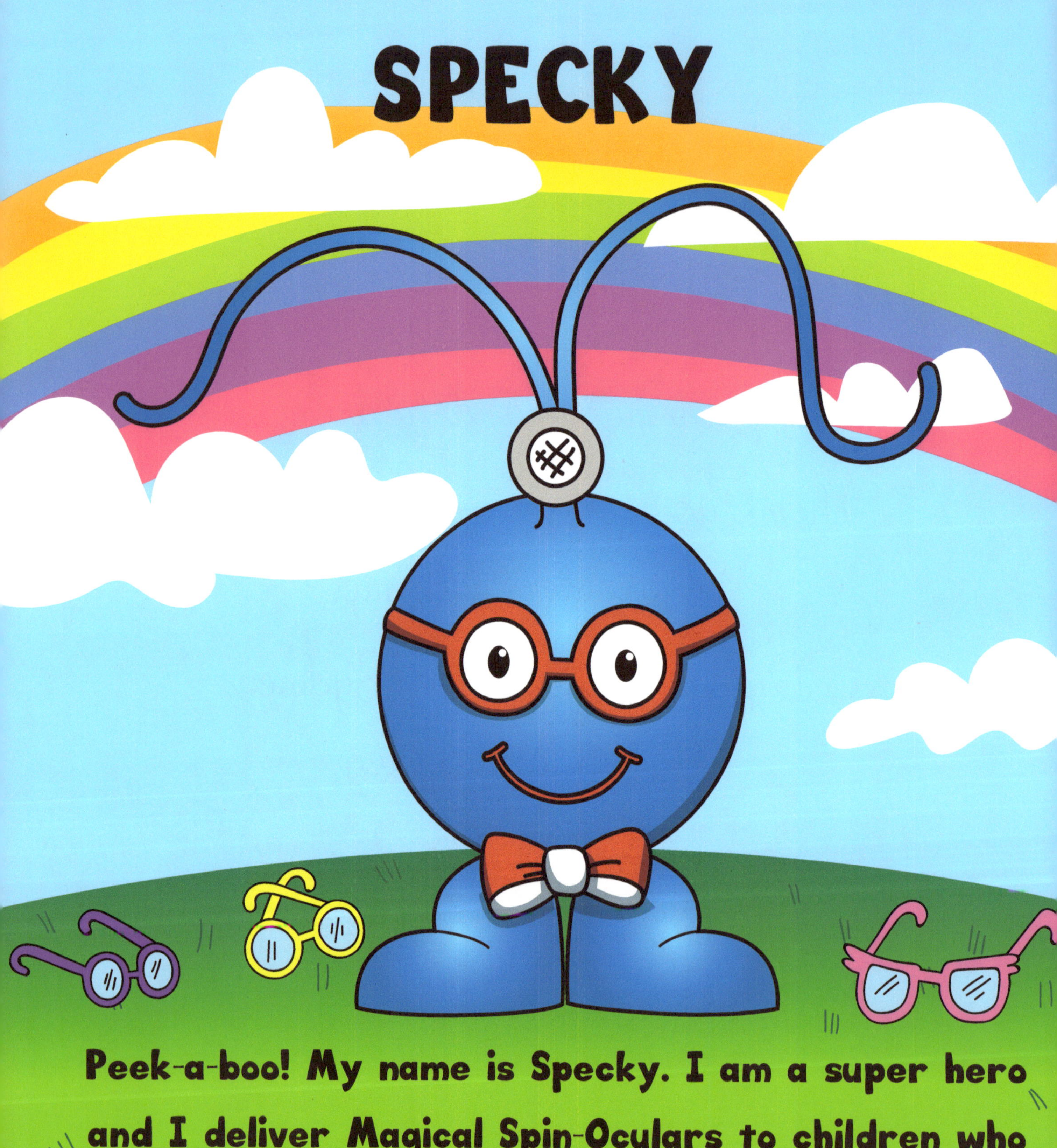

Peek-a-boo! My name is Specky. I am a super hero and I deliver Magical Spin-Oculars to children who are not behaving properly. When they put on a pair of Spin-Oculars, they can see the proper way to behave.

I like helping children make the
right choice. I fly upside down
and I like being silly. Wooty Woo!

SPECKLETTE

Hi, my name is Specklette.

I love making hearts and wearing them.

Can you find the three hearts I'm wearing?

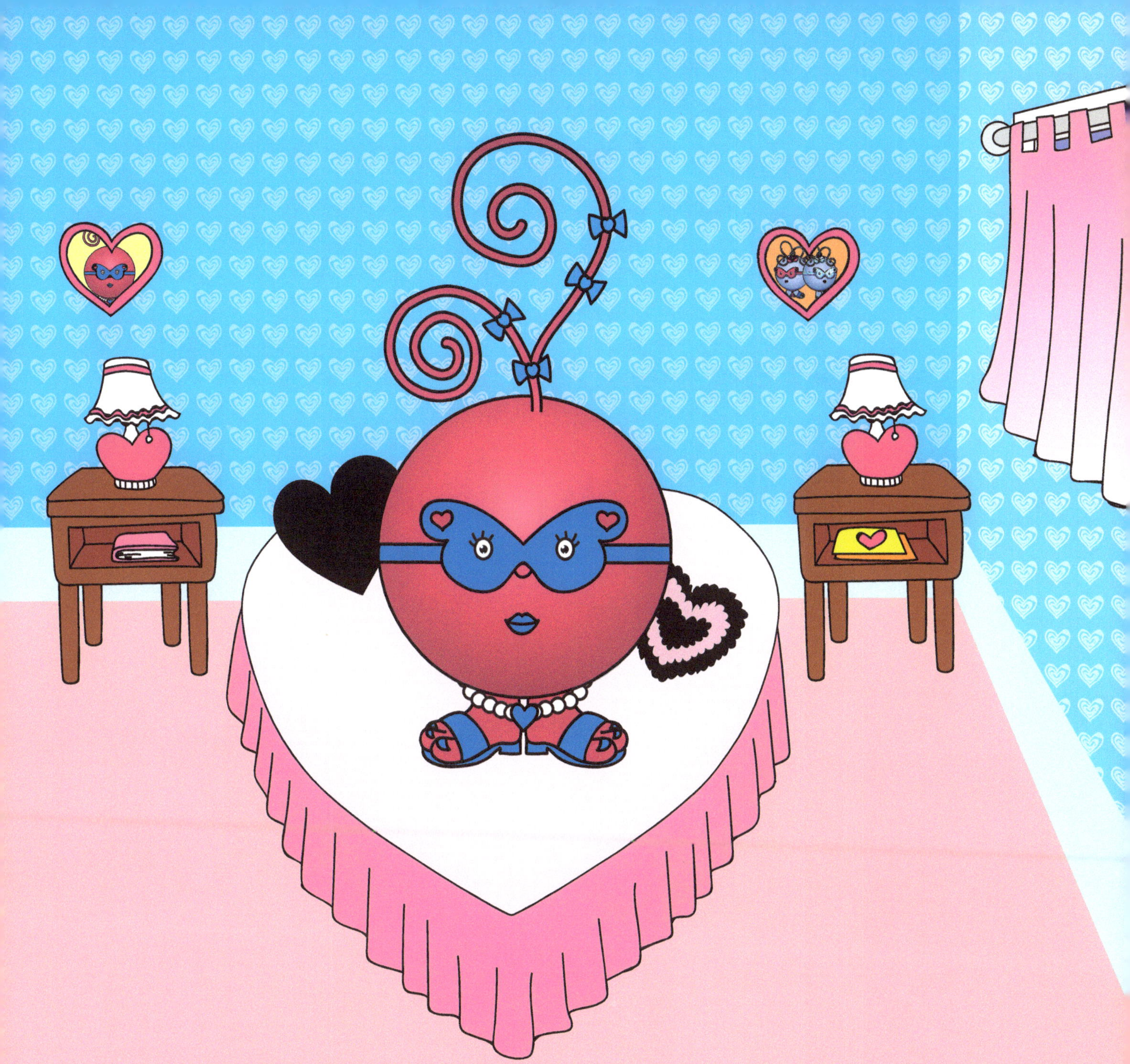

I love to eat Pinkleberries to keep
me pink and pretty. Bye bye.

SPARKLES & SPECKLES

Hi. Hee hee, we are twin sisters.

My name is Sparkles. And my name is Speckles.

Specklette is our Mommy and we love to make

heart-shaped cookies with her.

We love going to Peach Beach with Mommy every day to play in the sand and sing and dance. Bye bye.

CRABBY WABBY & SNAILEY HAILEY

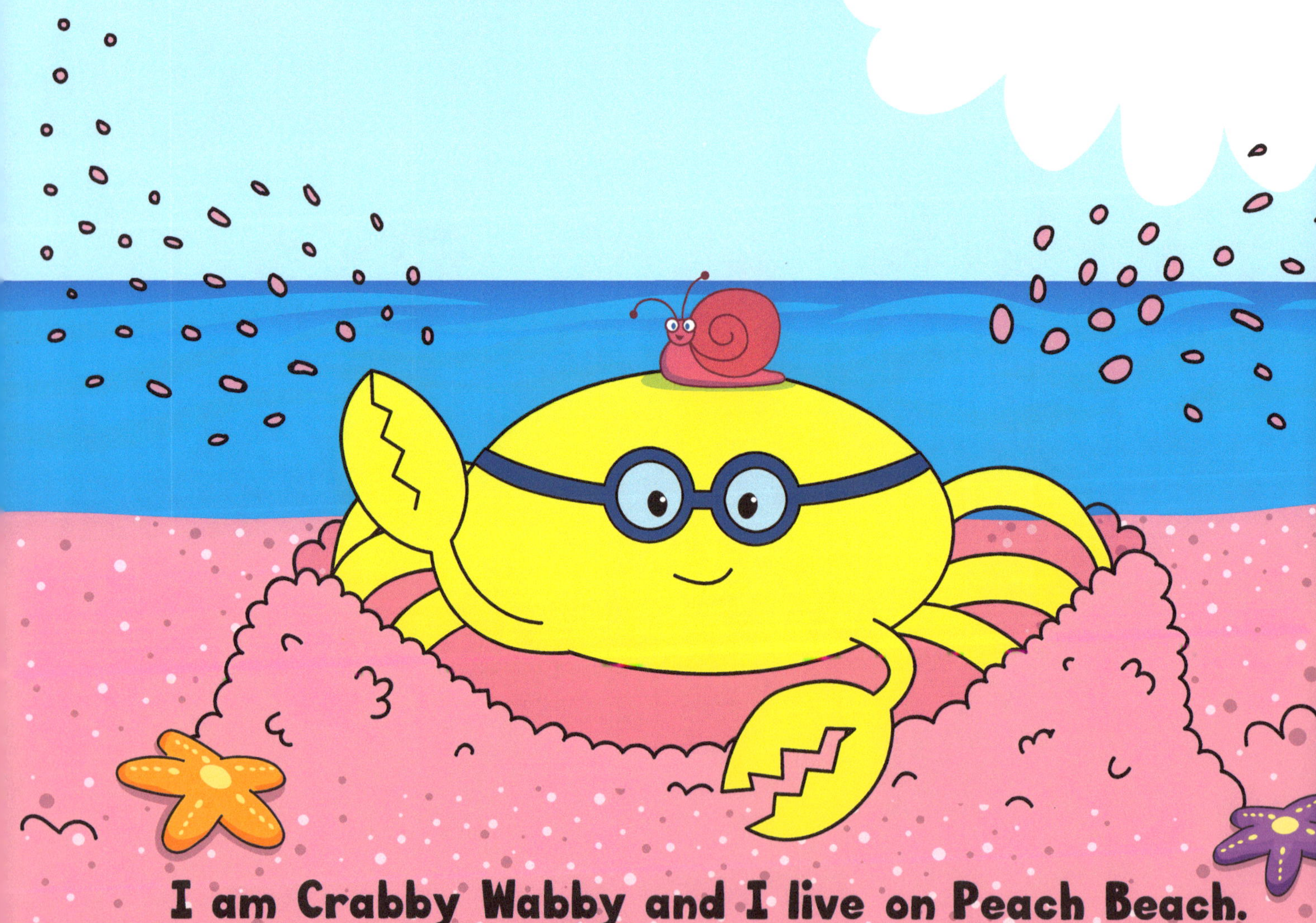

I am Crabby Wabby and I live on Peach Beach. I love to dig deep in the sand every day and make great big holes. My friends tell me I am always crabby. I gotta go dig dig dig.

Hi hi, my name is Snailey Hailey
and I am Crabby Wabby's best friend.
I live on Peach Beach.
I pop out of my shell and
put on a show every day.

I love to sing very loud so everyone
can sing along and dance.
LAAA LAA LAA!

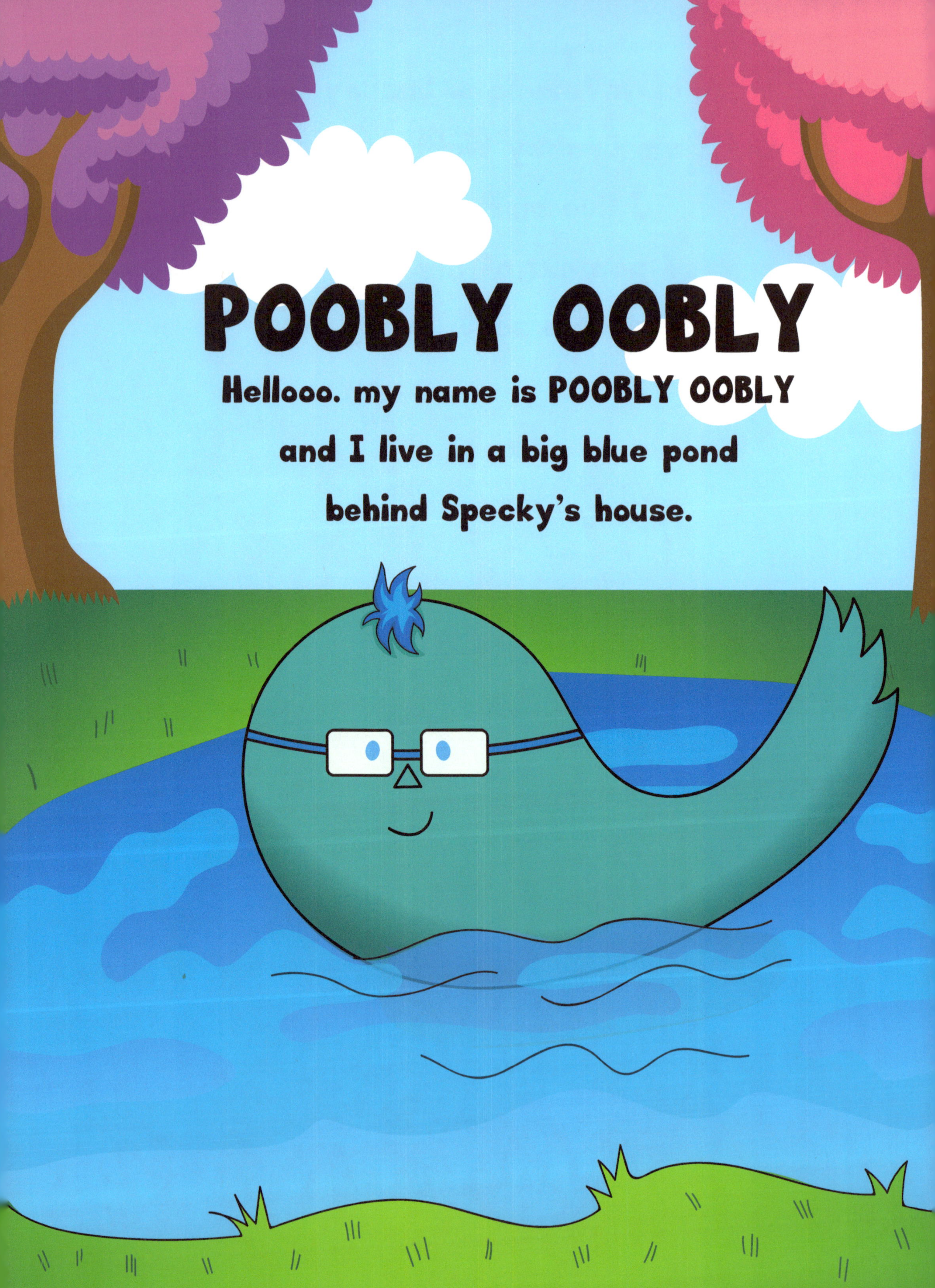

POOBLY OOBLY
Hellooo. my name is POOBLY OOBLY
and I live in a big blue pond
behind Specky's house.

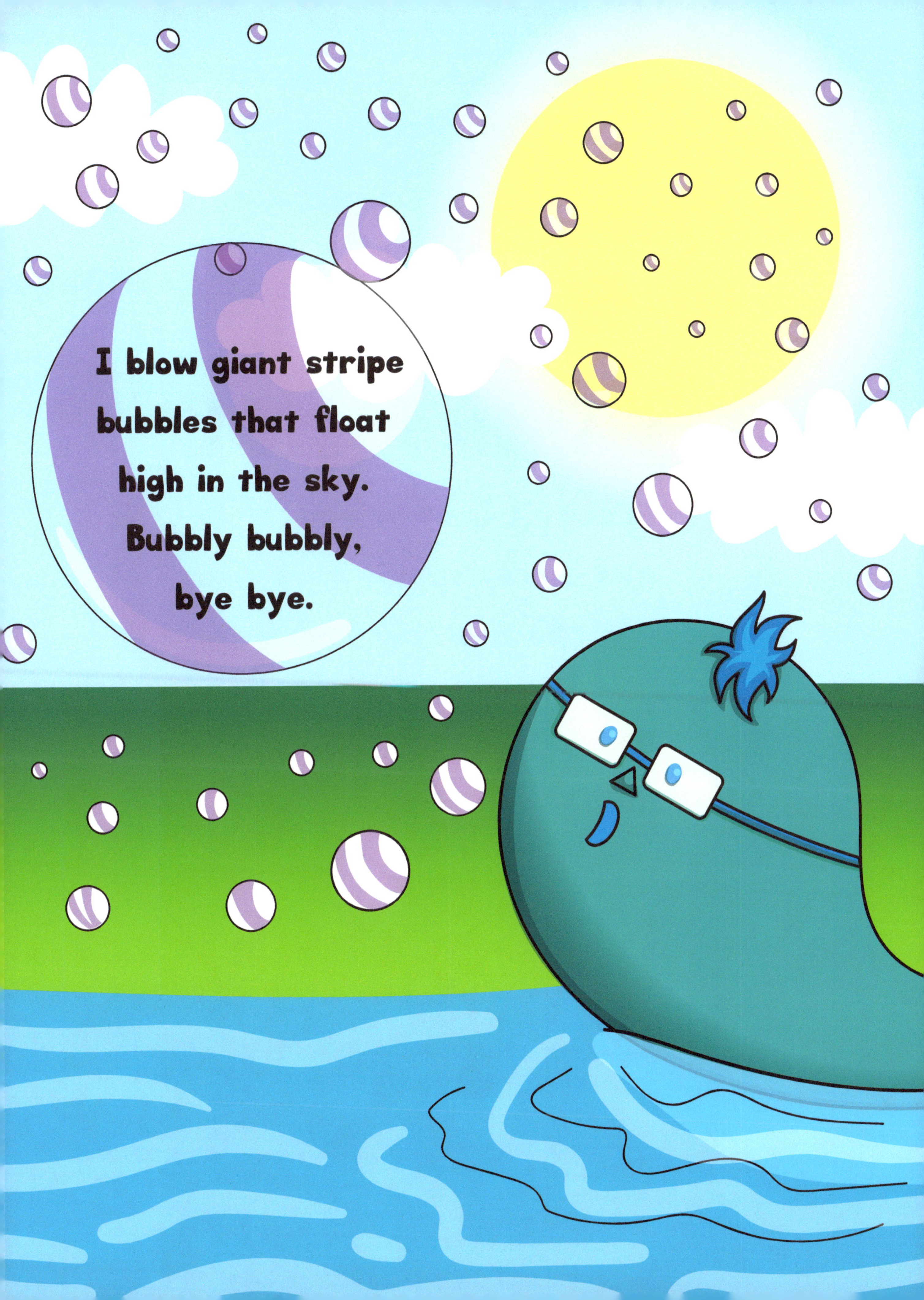

I blow giant stripe
bubbles that float
high in the sky.
Bubbly bubbly,
bye bye.

WORRY WOE

I am Specky's best friend, Worry Woe,

and I only speak in rhymes.

So now you know.

I help him deliver Spin-Oculars
and stick my tongue out as we go.

SPIFFIT
Mawow, my name is Spiffit.
I am Sparkle's and Speckle's pet.

I love to whistle, but when I sneak
and eat too many lemonberries,
my lips blow up and I can't whistle.
Ha ha, bye bye.

FOOFY OOFY

Hi hi hi, I am an itty-bitty bird.

I can only hop
and barely fly.
Bye bye.

SPOODLES

Hello, my name is Spoodles. I live in the hidden wonderland, the special place where Specky comes to make Magical Spin-Oculars.

I love daisies.
Can you find all the
daises I am wearing?

BLUR

Boo! I am Blur, a mean villain. I always try to stop Specky from delivering the Magical Spin-Oculars to children. Whenever I walk I bounce up and down because my legs are like springs.

I don't even want to say goodbye to you.

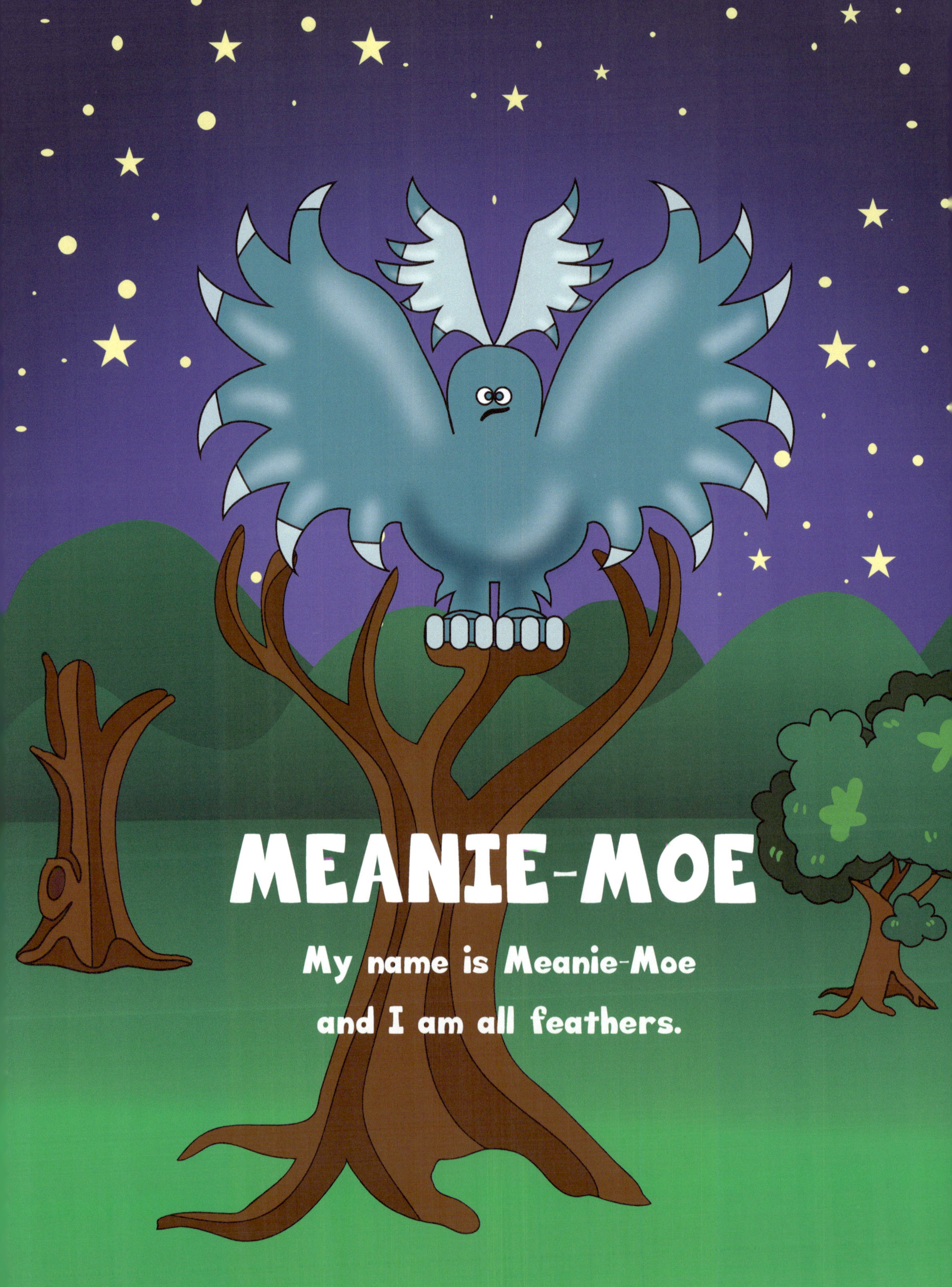

MEANIE-MOE
My name is Meanie-Moe
and I am all feathers.

Every time I fly, I have fire
coming out of my wings.
I am Blur's best friend and we
like being mean together. Bye.

SNIPS

My name is Snips. I have giant ears that make it easier for me to hear what everyone is talking about. Did I just hear you laugh at me?

I have magical powers
so I can become a banana,
a bicycle, a ball,
or anything I want to be.

DIGGLIN

My name is Digglin. I have shovels
for hands and a corkscrew nose.

I dig underground tunnels for Blur,
so when he is deep in the tunnel
you won't be able to see him.
Bye Zoom Ditty Zoom.

It was nice meeting you.
We can't wait to
see you again!

Just a few words about Specky and His Magical Spin-Oculars book series.

Tweedy Katz is a mother of identical twin daughters with extensive experience in early childhood education and a love for children. At the age of five, her twins were required to wear eye glasses. In the 1980s there was not a market for fashionable eye wear for children, which led to Tweedy's daughters being teased. Tweedy created a successful children's eyewear line, and an adorable blue character she called "Specky." He became the trademark for the company and is now the main character in her books. By the time her daughters went off to college, Tweedy created 14 additional fun-loving characters, all of which enhance and embrace joy, peace, and kindness.

The series of books she has written make children happy while providing them with positive messages. Tweedy's books are always filled with fun, learning, and delightful, vibrant characters for the whole family to enjoy!

www.spinoculars.com

"Children should be kissed, loved, heard, and cherished." –Tweedy Katz

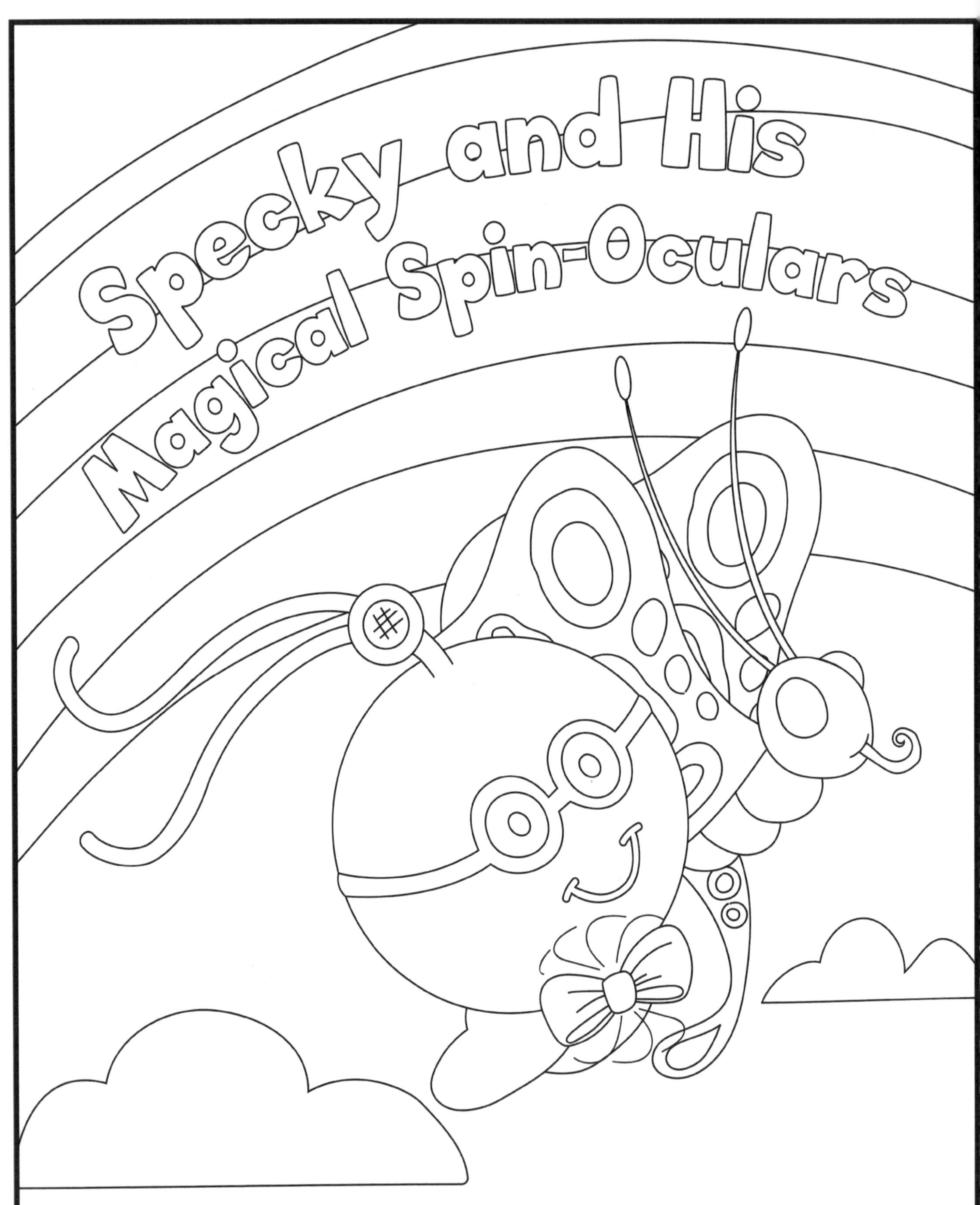

Have fun coloring Specky and Worry Woe

Specky and His Magical Spin-Oculars
Helping Chunkee

Written by Tweedy Katz
Illustrated by Tweedy Katz & Leslie Braginsky

Specky flies as fast as he can to deliver Magical Spin-Oculars to children—and wait till you see what happens next! This fully illustrated book for ages 3–8, *Specky and His Magical Spin-Oculars: Helping Chunkee,* tells the story of how Specky is teased as a child because he has to wear glasses. When Specky grows up, he decides to make and deliver Magical Spin-Oculars to children who are not behaving properly. That's when Specky becomes a *Super Hero.*

Chunkee is very sad and needs a pair of Magical Spin-Oculars to help him to see there is something else to do besides sit at his computer all day and miss meals with his mommy and daddy. Specky delivers the Magical Spin-Oculars to Chunkee. What will Chunkee do when he puts them on?

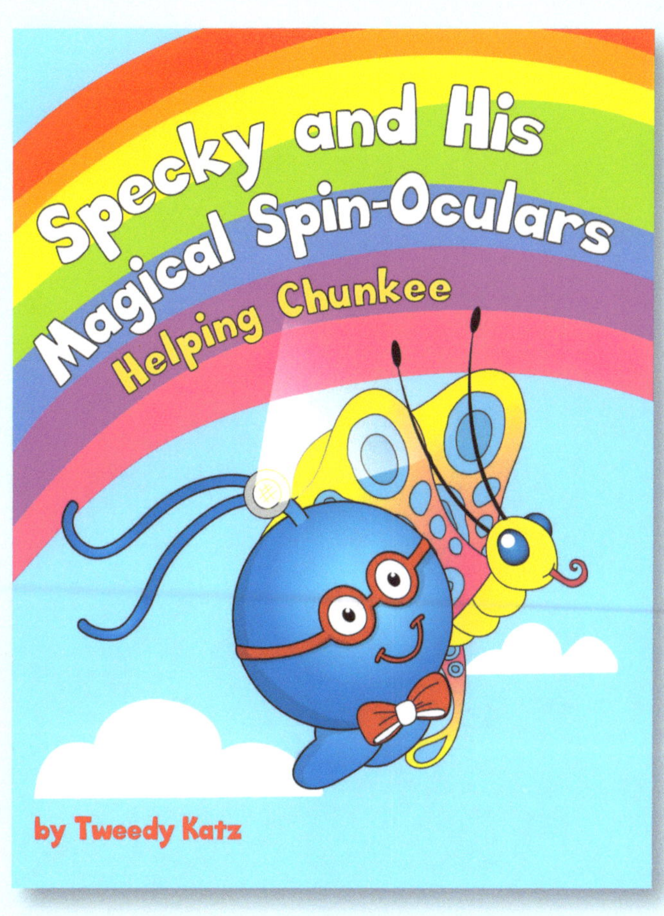

Author Tweedy Katz takes young children on a fun journey with Specky as he finds a way to remind children that there is a difference between proper and inappropriate behavior. This well-written, inspiring story delivers a fun learning message to children, complemented by vibrant, delightful characters and illustrations. This story is enjoyable for the whole family as well!

For more information or to purchase autographed copies, visit: www.Spinoculars.com